T0152418

Sense and Sensibility

A Lenten Exploration

SAM PORTARO

CHURCH
PUBLISHING
INCORPORATED

Unless otherwise noted, the Scripture quotations contained herein are from the New Revised Standard Version Bible, copyright © 1989 by the Division of Christian Education of the National Council of Churches of Christ in the U.S.A. Used by permission. All rights reserved.

Page 4 (puddle jumping): photo by Jeff Portaro, used by permission; page 34 (Trompe l'oeil): photo by Sam Portaro, mural by Richard Haas, used by permission; page 54 (swinging thurible): photo by Br. Michael Francis (Scott Smith), used by permission of churchartphotography.com; page 74 (Maddie Agnes & Otis Campbell-Lucas): photo by Steward Lucas and Doug Campbell, used by permission; all other photos by Sam Portaro.

Church Publishing
19 East 34th Street
New York, NY 10016
www.churchpublishing.org

Cover design by Jennifer Kopec, 2Pug Design
Typeset by PerfecType, Nashville, Tennessee

Library of Congress Cataloging-in-Publication Data

Names: Portaro, Sam Anthony, author.
Title: Sense and sensibility : a Lenten exploration / Sam Portaro.
Description: New York, NY : Church Publishing, [2018]
Identifiers: LCCN 2018030845 (print) | LCCN 2018035949 (ebook) | ISBN
    9781640651289 (ebook) | ISBN 9781640651272 (pbk.)
Subjects: LCSH: Lent--Meditations. | Senses and sensation--Religious
    aspects--Christianity--Meditations.
Classification: LCC BV88 (ebook) | LCC BV88 .P67 2018 (print) | DDC
    242/.34--dc23
LC record available at https://lccn.loc.gov/2018030845

Printed in Canada

CONTENTS

INTRODUCTION

L ent is often a season given to denial of physical pleasure and sensation. Yet a cultural atmosphere saturated with visual images, noise and air pollution, violence, and processed foods has dulled the senses.

Physical sensation plays an integral role in the human capacity for emotion and feeling. Overstimulation of the senses gradually erodes one's ability to feel emotionally. Empathy—emotional identification and connection with others—is crucial to liturgical engagement, especially in the highly dramatic practices of the signal events of the Christian Year.

The discipline of a forty-day preparation for Easter suggests the importance that the Church places on this seasonal retelling of the central acts of Christian redemption. A renewed relationship with our physical *senses* is prerequisite to a *sensibility* deeply attuned to engagement with the biblical

stories read, taught, and liturgically reenacted in the rites of
Ash Wednesday, Palm Sunday, Holy Week, and Easter.

These pages revisit the five physical senses—one per
week—in Lent. An introductory essay on Ash Wednesday,
and reflections on the Thursday, Friday, and Saturday thereafter, address the role of the senses in the experience and
expression of human compassion, the essential component
for engaging and participating in the liturgies of Holy Week
and Easter. These liturgies invite us to enter and engage the
scriptural stories that form the central tenets of Christian
faith in one's heart, soul, and life.

The following information may be especially helpful
to those responsible for teaching and preaching, especially
at weekday services throughout the Lenten season, and
to individuals who choose to use this series for personal
enrichment.

Essay reflections on each of the Sundays in Lent take up
one of the five senses: sight, sound, smell, touch, and taste.
While no attempt has been made to link the Sunday entries
to the Sunday eucharistic lectionary (RCL), the creative
homilist may find resources here. However, the intent of the
Sunday reflections is to prepare for the week ahead.

Daily reflections are frequently framed by either a portion from the collect for the day, and/or one or more of the
readings appointed for the "Weekdays in Lent" as found in
Weekday Eucharistic Propers (New York: Church Publishing,

2017, pp. 12ff.) and in most editions of *Lesser Feasts and Fasts*. While it is not necessary to follow the lectionary, the practice is recommended and may be especially helpful in crafting homilies.

Palm Sunday begins Holy Week and the reflection for that day is a prologue to engagement with the events that follow in the liturgical drama. Reflections on the days thereafter, including Easter, focus on the Passion narrative, referencing the physical senses when appropriate, but turning the attention, as is proper, to the biblical story at the heart of this season.

ASH WEDNESDAY AND THE DAYS FOLLOWING

[Y]ou are sealed by the Holy Spirit in Baptism and marked as Christ's own for ever.

(Holy Baptism, The Book of Common Prayer, page 308)

ASH
WEDNESDAY

When the sign of the cross is made in transparent oil on the forehead of the newly baptized, the recipient is thereby "marked as Christ's own forever." On Ash Wednesday, the first day of the season of Lent, the previously invisible signet is retraced in visible charcoal. Gritty ash is pressed into the pores of one's brow. The earlier affirmation is replaced with a sharp admonition:

"Remember that you are dust, and to dust you shall return."

This reminder of one's mortality can cast life in deep shadow, and for some this is the primary shade of Lent. Disciplines of self-denial are customary, occasionally relieved by periods of intentional self-giving, like volunteer service to those in need or similar works of kindness and mercy.

The rite impresses our mortality upon us. It literally rubs it in with that cruciform signature traced in ash on human skin.

Skin. It's the largest organ of the human body. And today—Ash Wednesday—it's touched and marked again as Christ's own forever.

So we begin Lent with this powerful reminder of our embodied life. The abrasive texture of the ash, the grinding action of this marking are like sandpaper drawn across the tender skin of the face and we're reminded that we're incarnations of the crucified and risen Christ. We have bodies, we *are* bodies. We're bodies endowed with senses.

Lent, then, isn't a time to deny the mortal body. Rather, Lent may be just the season to remember that we're mortal as dust and ash, and yet as such, we're graced in that mortality. Our very perishability only enhances our preciousness.

Thus, in this Lent we propose to explore more intently our embodied selves and the incarnate world we inhabit, that as we make our way through these forty days we come once again to our senses.

Thursday after
Ash Wednesday

Disembodied spirituality is antithetical to Incarnation and nigh impossible for us physical creatures. Seemingly intangible spiritual exercises of thought, meditation, and reflection are all dependent upon the tangible. Loving God with heart, mind, and strength is an organic undertaking. Yet so much of the sheer physicality of spirituality is overlooked, unconsidered—simply taken for granted.

Endowed with five physical senses, we tend to see these gifts merely as means to an end, as conduits of data, overlooking the inherent holiness of the sense itself. Just as we treat food as fuel, mindlessly ingesting food with little regard to its own integrity, so we absorb sensations with little appreciation for the sense that allows us to meet and mind the world around and within us. Just as each food is imbued with myriad properties of flavor, texture, and nutrition, so each sense is richly complex.

To limit "sensuality" to the realm of sex is to restrict the fullness of this word. Sensuality is pleasure in the physical. An integrated, embodied, incarnate spirituality fully pleasing to God and creature will delight in the sensate.

The season of Lent is an especially good time to embrace a heightened awareness—an intentional mindfulness—of the sensual. It's a good time to pay attention to the physical connections and conduits of daily life.

In a culture not-so-subtly pushing us into "virtuality," attention to and appreciation for the material ties of touch, taste, sight, sound, and smell are profound spiritual disciplines. Be mindful of the many wonders that greet and meet through sight, sound, smell, taste, and touch. In their collective daily dance, they embody and welcome us to a communion of the sensory, and the sensational.

FRIDAY AFTER
ASH WEDNESDAY

*Support us . . . Lord, with your gracious favor through
the fast we have begun; that as we observe it by bodily
self-denial, so we may fulfill it with inner sincerity of
heart. . . .*

(from the Collect for Friday after Ash Wednesday,
Lesser Feasts and Fasts, 2006, page 30)

B ut how shall we undertake a "fast" of "bodily self-
denial" and yet engage and enhance the sensual? Are
these practices not in opposition to one another?

Well, only to a degree. Throughout our lives we learn
that the limitations of our mortality demand that we must
often sacrifice one thing in order to obtain another. So it
is that if we're literally to come to our senses, we'll have to
clear a path.

And a messy, scattered path it is.

My senses are fenced off and held at bay by all manner of hindering obstacles. If I wish to hear the person addressing me—or just the wind in the trees—I must remove the earpieces pumping throbbing rhythms into my head, or put down the phone pressed to my temple, or simply silence my own voice.

If I want to smell fresh air gently dampened by the lake and warmed by the sun, I have to step outside the mall, beyond the heavily perfumed scents of the cosmetic counters. I have to get past the ventilation fans pumping the fragrances of garlic, popcorn, and hot grease into the alleys. I have to move beyond the grates that carry the subway's strange but unique musk and the sewer's stench to the street above.

In other words, I must *fast*.

I must abstain or absent myself from certain practices and places. As a right beginning, I regard more intently all those obstructions and intrusions that dull, distract, or distort my essential senses. What must I give up in order to gain the senses I seek?

SATURDAY AFTER
ASH WEDNESDAY

God, mercifully look upon our infirmities, and in all our dangers and necessities stretch forth your right hand to help and defend us. . . .

(from the Collect for Saturday after Ash Wednesday, *Lesser Feasts and Fasts*, 2006, page 31)

Only a few short hours before I opened the page to this prayer, I accompanied my husband on an errand. Multiple Sclerosis has compromised his balance and hobbled his poise. He walks haltingly with a cane, often slowly. As we crossed an intersection, he apologized that he couldn't walk better or faster. I assured him that I had no need or desire to be anywhere else any more quickly. Because he must keep his eyes on the ground at his feet lest he trip, my eyes are his periscope, alert to all around and above us. As the pianist "sees" the keys even while eyes are fixed on the printed score, I maintain vigil over his feet, conscious of his steps, ready to avert the stumble, offer the steadying hand or arm, or catch the possible fall.

As I grow more aware of all the obstructions and intrusions that dull, distract, or distort my essential senses, I'm soon aware also of what an overwhelming array it is.

My ears ring even when the loudest rackets are stilled; I've so long endured the noise that true silence is impossible. Tinnitus fills my head with the sonic pitches of myriad cicadas in sustained chorus. Definitely an infirmity, a legacy of my frail humanity.

Indoors or out, wherever my eye falls, it fills with images that demand, distract, and sometimes even delight. Dangers and necessities are commingled and thus all the more confusing. Which is which, and how shall I know the difference?

So I begin Lent with a prayer that reminds me I don't make this journey alone. I set out in the company of God, a beloved partner and friend who understands and makes allowance for my infirmities, who stands close enough to stretch out the protective hand in the reflexive split second it takes to fend off any danger or demand that threatens my balance, trips my stride, or tempts me to stray.

LENT 1

———

TOUCH

SUNDAY

My fingers, hands, and feet make contact with many surfaces as I move through a day's activities. Shoulders, hips, elbows, back, and butt are all points at which my body makes contact with the world as I sit and balance. Once lifted from the morning pillow, my head may settle gently in rest or suffer the occasional sharp, smarting blow, oscillating between these extremes in response to myriad directives and distractions as I navigate the day.

Touch is the sense—and medium—through which I most often encounter the spirited holy. This awareness came vividly on one of those incredibly gorgeous late summer mornings when every aspect of the world around me seemed in concert as I walked the full length of Lincoln Park, one of Chicago's loveliest and largest green expanses. A gentle but quite noticeable breeze blew through trees, grasses, and flowers and landed upon my bare arms, face, and legs like a passionate caress.

As a year-round walker, I am often accompanied by wind and though I seldom make the connection, on this particular morning the Hebrew word *ruach* came to mind. *Ruach* means "breath," or "spirit," and the gentle wind caressing me was a sudden reminder of the many ways I'm touched by this manifestation of God. Moreover, the wind reminded me that touch is not only how I actively connect with the world; it's also a way the world—and God—connect with me.

Touch is essential to an encounter with the spirited God; the very word "spirituality" is derived from and inextricably linked to a receptivity to touch. The silent, invisible God comes to us, communes with us, most often in and through the ability of our bodies and souls to be touched. Whether it's the physical sensation of wind, rain, or other element upon our skin, or the less tangible movement of emotions stirring deep within. When that rush of visual, audible, tangible, aromatic stimuli suddenly pierces, finds a route to our interior, arousing the host of emotions that give expression to feeling, we've been touched by the Holy.

MONDAY

I was hungry and you gave me food, I was thirsty and you gave me something to drink, I was a stranger and you welcomed me, I was naked and you gave me clothing, I was sick and you took care of me, I was in prison and you visited me. . . . [A]s you did it to one of the least of these who are members of my family, you did it to me.

(Matthew 25:35–36, 40)

This familiar teaching of Jesus in Matthew's Gospel is filled with touch. To feed the hungry, relieve the thirsty, welcome the stranger, clothe the vulnerable, and visit the captive, our bodies must be motivated. Hands and feet must move. The fulfillment of the gospel is hands-on.

And while it's inferred that these undertakings be directed to the needy, don't overlook Jesus's subtle reminder that wherever and whenever offered, these ministrations are given to all members of God's family.

Nearly every day I handle the ingredients that ultimately become our household meals; labor at writing that may nourish a hungry heart or relieve a thirsty soul; welcome others into relationship through mundane greetings that may lengthen into meaningful conversation; cover the open vulnerability of another with a sheltering word or an arm over a stooped shoulder or a friendly embrace; or sit within the confines of another's imprisonment, keeping company in their captivity until release is found.

Yes, it's laudable to venture afield in charity. But Jesus values also the many ways we touch the lives of those within our own families—the families we've made, and the families we've chosen—all bound up in God's expansive household.

TUESDAY

Pray then in this way:
Our Father in heaven,
hallowed be your name.
Your kingdom come.
Your will be done,
on earth as it is in heaven.
Give us this day our daily bread;
And forgive us our debts,
as we also have forgiven our debtors.

(Matthew 6:9–12)

For Jesus, prayer is physical. Not physical in the sense of pious posture. Physical in the sense of bodily activity.

If God's realm is to be realized, if God's will is to be manifest on earth as it is in heaven, bodies will be involved. Bodies that need bread to survive. Bread does not make itself; bread is the product of collaboration. God's Creation supplies the ingredients. Human hands make the meal.

Even forgiveness gets physical. My word of absolution is insufficient. I must make amends to those I have injured.

True prayer isn't just spoken, it's lived.

How then shall I pray today?

WEDNESDAY

When God saw what they did, how they turned from their evil ways, God changed his mind about the calamity that he had said he would bring upon them; and he did not do it.

(Jonah 3:10)

[J]ust as Jonah became a sign to the people of Nineveh, so the Son of Man will be to this generation.

(Luke 11:30)

[A] broken and contrite heart, O God, you will not despise.

(Psalm 51:18, The Book of Common Prayer,
page 267)

The story of Jonah, Nineveh, and God is so powerful it informs the belief of two families of faith—Jews and Christians. On this Wednesday in the first week of Lent, the story fills the eucharistic lectionary (Jonah 3:1–10, Luke 11:29–32) and is bridged by a resonant reading from the Psalter (Psalm 51:11–18).

The story of Jonah's experience in Nineveh—and of Nineveh's experience of Jonah—is filled with physical action. The plot depends, and the outcome demands, that Jonah physically go to Nineveh and engage personally with the people there.

But the crucial movement in the story isn't physical. It's emotional. The activity of Jonah and the response of Nineveh touched God. When God saw what the people of Nineveh did, God's mind and heart were changed and what God had intended and threatened to do, God chose not to do.

What have I done, what might I do today sufficient to touch God?

THURSDAY

Though the LORD be high . . .
he perceives . . . from afar.

> (Psalm 138:7, The Book of Common Prayer,
> page 793)

My doctor places his hands just so, and resting them gently, I feel the subtle pressure of one finger, then another. He's reading my body, his trained and experienced fingers searching out the hidden clues beneath.

A massage therapist presses her hands upon my leg. Her fingers quietly glide over the surface, kneading flesh and muscles. "You've been injured here," she says. The old wound left no visible scar, but her fingers see nonetheless.

The physician. The massage therapist. Each has a sense of touch so refined it's as though they're gifted with extra eyes, special eyes that can see what pupil, iris, cornea, and retina cannot.

Theirs is a special touch, unique to their vocations. But their touch reminds me that bodies are only outward and visible manifestations of lives bearing wounds and wonders hidden from my eyes. Though I may not possess their gift of fingers able to see, I am differently made. My eyes and ears, my mind and heart can sometimes detect the subtle hidden clues, the old hurts and unspoken joys—if I linger, and touch with mindful care.

FRIDAY

*Christ . . . grant us such fellowship in your sufferings,
that . . . we may subdue the flesh to the spirit, and the
spirit to you . . .*

(from the Collect for Friday in the First Week of
Lent, *Lesser Feasts and Fasts*, 2006, page 36)

Fellowship in sufferings. The technical term is *empathy*,
I suppose. Or perhaps something more.

Upon first meeting someone for whom I cared deeply
and with whom I shared many years of my life, my mother
was cool. Initially, I read her reserve as discomfort, a social
awkwardness in a new and challenging situation. As years
passed and the reserve remained, she came to speak of it.
She was at first perplexed, then stressed to tears that she
couldn't express more warmth for someone so obviously
important to me. "I just can't hug him," was all she could say.

What she didn't know, yet keenly fathomed, was a profound and painful brokenness at the heart of that relationship. Beneath the calm surface of our shared life, that partner and I were struggling. We were working at healing an infirmity marked by a breach of essential trust that brought suffering to us both, and that would eventually alter our relationship profoundly. Despite our sincere attempt to be reconciled and whole, my mother felt more deeply. She shared a fellowship in our sufferings.

Whatever else it may mean to "subdue the flesh to the spirit," in this instance it meant that I must remain silent. I couldn't disclose my private pain any more than any should ever know the awful agonies endured by Jesus, and by God, in their deepest sufferings. We cannot wrap our minds and hearts around those realities any more than my mother could embrace the one who was breaking my heart.

Yet it is enough, that fellowship in sufferings. Keeping company while respecting the private pain. Sharing without touching, until we all attain to the glory of Resurrection, when all that divides is done, all enmities are ended, and even enemies embrace.

SATURDAY

You have heard that it was said, "You shall love your neighbor and hate your enemy." But I say to you, Love your enemies and pray for those who persecute you, so that you may be children of your Father in heaven; for he makes his sun rise on the evil and on the good, and sends rain on the righteous and on the unrighteous. For if you love those who love you, what reward do you have? Do not even the tax collectors do the same? And if you greet only your brothers and sisters, what more are you doing than others? Do not even the Gentiles do the same? Be perfect, therefore, as your heavenly Father is perfect.

(Matthew 5:43–48)

Be perfect, as God is perfect. That's not a mandate. It's a clarification. What distinguishes the Christian? The Christian is remarkable for passionate, abiding commitment to reconciliation.

This admonition to "be perfect, as God is perfect" lost something essential in translation. It could also be rendered, "Be whole, as God is whole." In context, then, we're commended to a radical reconciliation, a commitment to wholeness such as we see in God.

Jesus was a toucher—couldn't, wouldn't keep his hands to himself. It got him into all kinds of trouble. He touched the unclean, the unholy, the good, the bad, and the ugly. Because he longed to bring it all together, to restore the family. Not just the cute ones, and the agreeable ones. Not only the envied cousins, but the wastrel brother and the wayward sister. If you're faced with a shattered mess, you've got to gather it all up to make it whole. You can't be whole by part. Gotta grasp it all, get your arms around it, and hold tight.

The world is flying apart, one person at a time. Fragmented, atomized, divided and conquered by social, religious, political, racial, digital barriers and walls we've yet to devise. Don't just stand there waiting for the pretty, the clean, the nice. God loves it all. For God's sake, reach out. Touch. Grasp. And hold on tight.

LENT 2

~

SIGHT

SUNDAY

Light is God's first gift of Creation. Light pierces the darkness of mystery. The God previously hidden in that mysterious darkness boldly initiates a process of self-revelation.

Seeing is believing, we say. Comprehension is signified in the expression, "I see."

But in our modern culture, we're bombarded with images. Moreover, our ability to manipulate and alter those images makes it all the more difficult to determine verifiable fact from visual fiction. Thus we're left with the burden of discerning truth.

I wake every morning to a visual reminder of this reality. It's a building only one block from our residence, clearly visible from our bedroom window. Most Chicagoans know this landmark. The structure boasts distinctive bays, ornamented with white glazed terracotta trim. Massed limestone on the lower levels is lightened by warm brick above. The central tier is crowned with a round oculus wreathed in carved relief. On either end of the building, an ornate portal of concentric arches recedes to entrance doors set into the wall beneath them. The narrow wall rising above the doors reveals subtle bas relief in bricks arranged in rectangles of varied depth and a single row of "Chicago windows"—windows with a large fixed center pane flanked by narrower double-hung sashes, a style pioneered here in this city. At the top of each end wall the oculus is repeated but enlarged and made all the more impressive by an elaborate frame of white terra cotta in the manner of Louis Sullivan.

The structure was a hotel when built in 1929, later converted to an apartment building. Nearly all the architectural detail I have described is a massive mural, a tribute to Chicago architecture, the design of artist Richard Haas, painted in 1980 and restored in 2005. The technical term is *trompe-l'œil*, in French meaning "deceive the eye."

Things are seldom exactly as they seem. Discernment demands attention to all that meets the eye, a healthy skepticism, perhaps even outright suspicion. People are more complicated than grooming, dress, and demeanors might suggest. A telescope opens out to deep heavens beyond our most distant stars, yawning infinity. A microscope reveals ecologies alive within a dust mote. Our universe is a multilayered thing of awesome complexity so vast no human eye can see it all, no mind encompass it entirely.

Wherever the eye falls there lies sufficiency for a life's meditation. Look. Then look again. And again. Let the gaze linger long, reach deep.

Seeing isn't believing; it's only the beginning.

MONDAY

Be merciful, just as your Father is merciful. Do not judge, and you will not be judged; do not condemn, and you will not be condemned. Forgive, and you will be forgiven; give, and it will be given to you.

(Luke 6:36–38a)

I've never been a poker player; that's probably a good thing. I don't have a poker face. My face tends to register too often and too vividly what's going on in my head. It's a trait I inherited from my late mother. It very likely came as part of the genetic package that also makes me a pretty big "J" on the Myers-Briggs scale. That means that I tend to form judgments quickly.

This trait can be helpful in some instances. But in other situations—especially in those complex occasions when I need to see the many perspectives of a person or a

predicament—I have to work hard at remaining open. I have
to suspend my judgment until I have sufficient information
to make an informed opinion.

We human beings are complex creatures. What we reveal
outwardly to the world is, like the proverbial iceberg, only
the tiny visible tip of a larger, deeper mass. Today's Gospel
first admonishes us to be merciful in the same ways and to
the same extent that God is merciful. Then it goes on to the
issues of judgment, condemnation, and forgiveness.

God sees and knows not only the visible tip of my life,
but sees also the hidden depths and dark masses beneath;
and yet God still extends full mercy to me, loving me and
forgiving me even in the full knowledge of who and what I
am. Who, then, am I to render anything less than mercy to
those I meet on life's journey?

Whatever I see of any other person—even one observed
as closely and dearly as a spouse or sibling—is too scant to
form any informed judgment. Specific acts may elicit and
deserve some attentive response, but the whole person—the
Child of God I am pledged in Baptism to respect and honor,
but see only in part—I'm incompetent to judge.

It's a discipline, and a hard one, to keep my eyes, my
heart, and my face open to receive.

TUESDAY

Then Jesus said to the crowds and to his disciples, "The scribes and the Pharisees sit on Moses's seat; therefore, do whatever they teach you and follow it; but do not do as they do, for they do not practice what they teach. They tie up heavy burdens, hard to bear, and lay them on the shoulders of others; but they themselves are unwilling to lift a finger to move them. They do all their deeds to be seen by others; for they make their phylacteries broad and their fringes long. They love to have the place of honor at banquets and the best seats in the synagogues, and to be greeted with respect in the marketplaces, and to have people call them rabbi. . . . All who exalt themselves will be humbled, and all who humble themselves will be exalted.

(Matthew 23:1–7, 12)

God . . . [d]eliver us when we are tempted to regard sin without abhorrence, and let the virtue of [Christ's] passion come between us and our mortal enemy.

(from the Collect for Tuesday in the Second Week of Lent, *Lesser Feasts and Fasts*, 2006, page 39)

Portions from both today's Gospel and collect turn us to examine the other side of sight: appearances—what we choose to show the world. This is that treacherous territory where, as the collect expresses it, "we are tempted to regard sin without abhorrence." And that's putting it mildly.

More often my concern with appearance encourages me to disregard entirely the sinful exercise of falsely representing my real self before the world. That was what Jesus condemned in the Pharisees he targeted as example. They could hardly have been blind to the blatant contradiction of their teachings and their actions. They simply assumed that either what they taught did not apply to them, or worse, that those whom they taught were stupid.

In this age and culture, where images are fashioned and messages are spun to the advantage of some and the detriment of many, as believers in the God of Truth do we not have an obligation to present ourselves honestly?

The collect names the foe "our mortal enemy." Less poetic, but certainly more clearly rendered, the enemy is ego. So for clarity's sake, I'll walk today with this version: God, when I'm tempted to make myself appear other than who I truly am, let the full reality of Christ's costly witness to the Truth of all You are step between me and the egotistical image in my mirror; that I may fully and honestly remember that always and everywhere, it's a sin to tell a lie.

WEDNESDAY

God . . . [g]rant that we, loving you above all things, may love our friends in you, and our enemies for your sake. . . .

(from the Collect for Wednesday in the Second Week of Lent, *Lesser Feasts and Fasts,* 2006, page 40)

While Jesus was going up to Jerusalem, he took the twelve disciples aside by themselves, and said to them on the way, "See, we are going up to Jerusalem, and the Son of Man will be handed over to the chief priests and scribes, and they will condemn him to death; then they will hand him over to the Gentiles to be mocked and flogged and crucified; and on the third day he will be raised."

Then the mother of the sons of Zebedee came to him with her sons, and kneeling before him, she asked a favor of him. And he said to her, "What do you want?" She said to him, "Declare that these two sons of mine will sit, one at your right hand and one at your left, in your kingdom." But Jesus answered, "You do not know what

you are asking. Are you able to drink the cup that I am
about to drink?" They said to him, "We are able." He said
to them, "You will indeed drink my cup, but to sit at my
right hand and at my left, this is not mine to grant, but it
is for those for whom it has been prepared by my Father."

(Matthew 20:17–23)

There are none so blind as those who will not see, declares the adage. In this excerpt from today's Gospel, Jesus even pointedly prefaces his words with the directive, "See." But apparently the picture Jesus painted was beyond their imagining. James and John, the sons of Zebedee, and their mother obviously saw a different outcome, a more pleasing prospect.

Salome, the mother of James and John, and perhaps a sister of Jesus's mother, Mary, sees the cost of what Jesus proposes. Perhaps acting upon her natural maternal concern, she trades upon relationship to secure comparable reward for her sons, blind to the conflict between such favoritism and the principles of justice and fairness Jesus has consistently taught and maintained. She doesn't see that her request undermines Jesus, making her an unwitting "enemy" to Jesus's vocation and mission. Neither she nor her sons see the conflict. Nor do they see that what they are asking isn't for Jesus to grant, that neither the reward nor consequence of sacrifice is guaranteed—that faith is *trust* and to share this specific cup is to share the risk of ultimate faith.

Sight is sometimes arbitrary. Two people scanning the clouds may see very different images. Imagination can enhance or distort reality. We're offered multiple possibilities in nearly every image and instance we encounter. Discernment often requires that we examine several possibilities to determine the truth.

Perhaps that's why the collect today encourages us to "love our friends in [God], and our enemies for [God's] sake." Until I look with God's eyes, I may not clearly see how to love my friends or my enemies as I ought, nor may I see that my perceived friends and enemies are not always as they seem, and may not be friends or enemies at all.

What shall I choose to see? Whom and how shall I love?

THURSDAY

There was a rich man who was dressed in purple and fine linen and who feasted sumptuously every day. And at his gate lay a poor man named Lazarus, covered with sores, who longed to satisfy his hunger with what fell from the rich man's table; even the dogs would come and lick his sores.

(Luke 16:19–21)

Indigent street petitioners are a familiar sight in most cities. Some are well known in their familiar locations, even greeted by name as members of the neighborhood. Others are only temporary or erstwhile visitors. But their presence is so familiar that many are seemingly invisible, or at least treated as such, either intentionally shunned or ignored by passersby too preoccupied to notice. They are unseen.

The story of Lazarus, a street person, and Dives, a man of means, is the Gospel portion today (Luke 16:19–31). It's a more complicated story when one realizes that there's no indication that either man, Lazarus or Dives, communicates with the other. Thus we're left to assumptions, and those aren't always reliable.

It seems to me that at the least Dives could have greeted, acknowledged, and perhaps have learned more of Lazarus, the man who sat by his gate. Lazarus, too, might likewise have reached out to Dives. There was risk to each man in each option.

What remains clear, however, is the very real chasm between Lazarus and Dives that endures beyond this life to the next, where its impassability becomes permanent, suggesting that the only bridges available to either character are in the here and now.

When I see and acknowledge the humanity in the other person, I take the first step toward relationship, the bridge across the chasm.

FRIDAY

Grant . . . Lord, that . . . we may have grace to forgive those who wrongfully or scornfully use us, that we ourselves may be able to receive your forgiveness.

(from the Collect for Friday in the Second Week of Lent, *Lesser Feasts and Fasts*, 2006, page 42)

The story of Joseph (Genesis 37:3–4, 12–28) and the parable of the vineyard (Matthew 21:33–43) recount stories of trust betrayed. Jacob's confidence in his sons and Joseph's reliance upon his brothers are disappointed in a tale of attempted fratricide. An unidentified vineyard owner analogous to God entrusts his holdings to tenant associates who mutiny, killing first those sent to collect the profits, then assassinating the second collector, the owner's son.

Despite the treacherous and tragic elements of these stories, each ends in forgiveness and reconciliation. How one gets through the thickets of wickedness to those happier endings is the grace for which we pray in today's collect.

It's a grace, and a discipline, to see beyond one's personal pain. Joseph might well have nursed an eternal enmity for his murderous brothers. God could certainly have abandoned the Creation project well before the Crucifixion. The grace extended in each instance required that the one wronged see beyond the pain and thus see the wrongdoers differently.

Perhaps Joseph came to see how his father's preferential affection, and his own tendencies to revel in that limelight, bred his siblings' jealousy. God certainly sees us and our world differently than we do, and with a patience beyond our comprehending.

Can I see beyond the perceived injustices and insults that breed resentment, jealousy, and a host of destructive emotions? Can I see more clearly the way to reconciliation with those who have injured me?

SATURDAY

[W]hile he was still far off, his father saw him and was filled with compassion; he ran and put his arms around him and kissed him.

(Luke 15:20)

My siblings are all younger than me and often perceived a difference in the way my mother related to me. "You'll always be her little boy," they said, right up to her death.

There's an element of truth in their assessment. Not only was I firstborn, but my mother's pregnancy was particularly stressful, owing to my father's near death. Had he not survived a very risky surgery, I'd have been her only child of a marriage just a year old.

To some extent I suppose each child is seen by a parent from perspectives and in ways denied any other. A parent sees not only the child, but the prehistory, every stage and passage shared, and a host of hopes still gestating in potential.

That's why I'm drawn to the image of that Prodigal Father/God whose vision remains consistent, regardless the vantage. No doubt the father of the parable saw his troublesome son with the same compassion even when they were fully apart. When the son's return is still so distant as to be imperceptible to everyone else, the father saw his own.

We are truly God's children. How else could God see us, except as the One who knows our prehistory, our every step up, every stumble down, and all we are yet to be, a sight to God's sore and weary but always compassionate eyes?

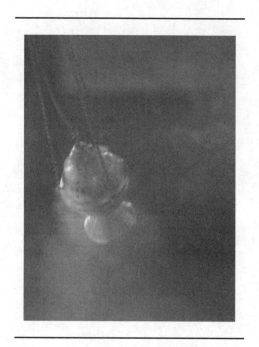

LENT 3

~

SMELL

SUNDAY

I was only five years old and I had fallen asleep on the long trip from Maryland to my maternal grandparents' house in North Carolina. It was dark as my father carried me through the door into a chilly unlighted room where the aroma of strong coffee woke me. We continued toward the outline of a door scribed in light, beyond which I heard voices. Dad leaned in and the spring hinges gave way to a bright, warm kitchen filled with people abuzz in conversation, fueled with the brew that had been percolating on the stove for who knows how long, waiting for our arrival. To this day, the rich smell of strong hot coffee in chilled air can sweep me back to that moment.

There are places and spaces I could still identify blindfolded. The old wood frame rural church that smelled of dust, mildew, aged hymnals, and red oil furniture polish. Our childhood home sheathed in brick with a concrete block foundation and musty basement always damp, built inside without plaster or sheetrock but entirely of wood that absorbed the scents of a large family housed, fed, and loved for nearly sixty years, attaining a distinctive musk. Small neighborhood Italian grocers where scents of parmesan, romano, salamis, and tomatoes simmered with abundant garlic, and hard-crusted peasant bread fresh from the oven begin to hint at my paternal grandmother's kitchen; add the acrid, sulfuric odor that permeated their coal-mining town in the hills of western Pennsylvania and the picture's complete.

Scent attracts and repels; the study of human pheromones is fascinating science, and very big business. Our noses help us identify friends and mates, and warn us of people and produce that may be a tad "off," or even poisonous. The incarnational power of scent is dramatically portrayed in the film *Brokeback Mountain*, when a grieving Ennis visits Jack's family home and finds momentary reunion with his deceased friend in the folds of a shirt.

Even the apostle Paul recognized that evangelism among many competing religions demanded a gospel that could pass the sniff test: "God . . . through us spreads in every place the fragrance that comes from knowing [Christ]. For we are the aroma of Christ to God. . . . [W]e are not peddlers of God's word like so many; but in Christ we speak as persons of sincerity, as persons sent from God and standing in his presence" (2 Corinthians 2:14–17).

While incense may have been introduced into the temple to mask the lingering odors of animal sacrifice, its usage—like its aroma—lingers as demarcation of holy space and a reminder that worship involves and engages all the senses—suggesting that perhaps even God appreciates an occasional nosegay.

An integrated spirituality includes an intentional consciousness, paying attention to the myriad means by which we meet God, one another, and new dimensions within ourselves through the senses, including the olfactory. Breathing sustains life, smell enlivens.

MONDAY

"Are not . . . the rivers of Damascus, better than all the waters of Israel? Could I not wash in them, and be clean?"

(2 Kings 5:12)

There were also many lepers in Israel in the time of the prophet Elisha, and none of them was cleansed except Naaman the Syrian.

(Luke 4:27)

The story of Naaman (2 Kings 5:1–15b; Luke 4:23–30) figures prominently in readings appointed for today. Though Naaman was held in high regard, valued for his military leadership in the army of Syrian king, Aram, he contracted leprosy. His disease may not have impaired his military skill or impeded his leadership on the battle-field, but there must have been some consequence to his infection. It was sufficient to send him to Israel in search of a cure, bearing a letter from his king to gain him access to Israel (where his disease may have prevented easy entry), and lavish gifts to reward his healer.

Naaman's response to Elisha's prescribed treatment—seven baths in the Jordan River—seems the height of ingratitude. If all he needed was seven baths, wouldn't the rivers of Syria have sufficed? Is his resistance rooted in political and social arrogance? Is he being fussy? It's unlikely that any waterways of that time were hygienically pristine.

Naaman's situation, and his insensitivity, may have been aggravated by the complicated relationship of his disease with the sense of smell. The bacterial infection and resulting lesions of leprosy often give off a distinctively noxious odor, all the more pronounced when personal hygiene is impeded by a scarcity of water. More importantly, one of the accompanying symptoms of leprosy is a loss of the leper's sense of smell.

Naaman's high standing and value to the realm may have shielded him from social shunning, and his own inability to detect the odors his body gave off may have insulated him from a thorough awareness of his own stink.

But if he was to be clean, Naaman had to put down his pride and take those baths.

Were he sainted, Naaman would be a patron of many, myself included. We are the ones whose own offenses are invisible to ourselves. We may reek, yet be impervious to our own noxiousness. Unless and until an Elisha dares to humiliate us into awareness.

Shall we gather at the river?

TUESDAY

[T]he hair of their heads was not singed, their tunics were not harmed, and not even the smell of fire came from them.

(Daniel 3:27)

Today's readings include a canticle associated with three young men with Hebrew names of Hananiah, Mishael, and Azariah. Also known by the Babylonian names, Shadrach, Meshach, and Abednego, the tale of how they were consigned to a fiery furnace for refusing to worship a golden idol was a familiar staple of the Bible storybooks of my childhood. Their piety under duress was a testament of faith, and their miraculous survival of the ordeal was convincing evidence that the God of Israel had no desire of burnt offerings of any kind—certainly not human!

But I can sympathize with our ancient ancestors who perceived a connection between prayer and smoke. The pleasing aromas emitted by roasting food, smoldering resins, steeping spices—and the visible upwards draft of diaphanous smoke or steam—have long been elements of devotion and worship.

In my teens I directed and accompanied a small choir for Sunday morning worship at the local Salvation Army post in town. The steadfast congregation of regulars followed a simple order of Wesleyan worship and sang hymns familiar to my Methodist roots. There was no incense, per se. But as we prayed and sang, the aromas of frying chicken, green beans flavored with fatback, biscuits, yeast rolls, cornbread, and cinnamon-laced apple pie drifted up from the kitchen below as workers prepared a meal for the hungry.

Prayers, praise, and the sweet smell of an abundant table all rose together. I don't know about the prayers and was never too sure about the music, but the savor of that food surely rejoiced the heart of God.

WEDNESDAY

*Lord . . . direct the way of your servants in safety . . .
amid all the changes of our earthly pilgrimage.*

(from the Collect for Wednesday in the Third Week
of Lent, *Lesser Feasts and Fasts*, 2006, page 46)

M y mother was a simple woman, born and reared on a farm in rural North Carolina. She and a sister undertook their greatest adventure together, moving in the 1940s to Washington, DC, where they eventually met the men they would marry.

I suspect it was in that city, at a big store like Woodward & Lothrop, that my mother first discovered "Tailspin," a fragrance named for the dangerous plummeting spiral of an airplane and sold under the name of French couturier, Lucien Lelong. It became her signature perfume and our father and we children would go to any lengths to locate it, for it was a gift guaranteed to please.

Though she seldom had occasion to wear it, because it was her favorite its fragrance eventually subtly permeated her clothes. And whether she'd spent the day hanging laundry on the lines or weeding the vegetable gardens outside, or canning fruits, baking cakes, preparing our meals and washing our dishes inside, whenever you put your arms around her and drew close, something of that perfume's aura was there.

When she died and we children gradually cleared the closets of their sad reminders, the one item of furniture our father declared off-limits was our mother's dresser. When our father died, I opened the topmost drawer.

Clothes and accessories remained as they'd been at her death nine years previous. But rising from the open drawer was the slightest hint of that signature fragrance we associated with "safety . . . amid all the changes of our earthly pilgrimage" and I understood profoundly why our father kept it close, within reach of the bed in which he passed from this life to the next.

THURSDAY

Keep watch over your church . . . Lord, with your unfailing love; and, since it is grounded in human weakness and cannot maintain itself without your aid, protect it from all danger. . . .

(from the Collect for Thursday in the Third Week of Lent, *Lesser Feasts and Fasts*, 2006, page 47)

The elevator rose as always and stopped at the nineteenth floor. Stepping into the hallway leading to our apartment, the strong smell of something burning concerned me; only the lack of any visible smoke restrained a real panic. As I approached our door the odor grew stronger, but the entry handle was cool and when I turned the key and pushed the door inward, the air beyond was clear. Dropping my bag, I turned, stepped back into the hall, and rapped our neighbor's brass knocker hard.

The door opened a few inches to reveal her embarrassment as she offered, "It's okay. I burned something on the stove" only minutes before three firemen in full gear, one bearing a large axe, rushed down the hall. On the street below, police barricaded the block at each end, and fire trucks stood bumper to bumper the full length between. Fire is serious business. In a high-rise building, it's deadly serious.

Someone—I never learned who—had obviously smelled the smoke and instinctively initiated the chain of communication that dispatched emergency respondents in an impressive testament to the power of the smell of danger.

A short while later, after things had quieted, I knocked gently on the neighbor's door and asked if she needed anything. She demurred, with thanks, then leaned against the jamb. She looked tired, and with reason; she worked hard, rising very early to open her business, ready to receive her customers by seven in the morning, and often not returning home till ten in the evening, or later. That night, she had come home, put some meat to cook on the stove for her dinner, and sat for only a brief moment, falling immediately into sleep, to wake with a start when the smoke reached her nostrils.

I am often critical of the institutional church; I'm well aware of its human foundations and acquainted with its vulnerability to all the consequences thereto. Today's collect is a reminder of that grounding "in human weakness" that leaves the Church, and us, in danger. But it's also a reminder that sometimes the danger and disasters we incur are not intentional, but accidental. They are the consequence of an inherent weakness, the consequence of simply being what God has made us to be: human.

The power of this prayer is its simultaneous absolution of those accidents beyond our sinful intent and its bold reminder to the Creator that there are consequences to that Creation, that not only we, but God, must "keep watch," be ever mindful and always vigilant—that Lent and its disciplines are not for us alone.

FRIDAY

[Israel] shall blossom like the lily,
he shall strike root like the forests of Lebanon.
His shoots shall spread out;
his beauty shall be like the olive tree,
and his fragrance like that of Lebanon.
They shall again live beneath my shadow,
they shall flourish as a garden;
they shall blossom like the vine,
their fragrance shall be like the wine of Lebanon.

(Hosea 14:5–9)

The portion of Hosea's prophesy appointed for today describes an imagined Israel fully restored to loving relationship with God. The images are heavily botanical: lily, olive tree, garden, blossom, vine. Reference is made several times to the fragrance of Lebanon, legendary for the redolent perfume of its towering cedars, olive trees, verdant gardens filled with the rich scent of lilies, and vineyards and orchards bearing fruit, yielding wines with full bouquet.

Winter in Chicago can be bracing. The most beautiful days of clear skies and rare bright sun are often the coldest, there being no blanket of low-hanging clouds to hold the scant warmth of earth closer. The air outside is crystal cold. It smells of ice, the olfactory equivalent of purest white.

The cold is like a palate cleanser, preparing the nasal receptors for a new smell. Stepping into a grocery, the specific aroma of nearly every item of fresh produce displayed seems to rise and greet one's approach. Entering a flower shop, fragrance races color and often wins, reaching the brain first.

In contrast to the sacrificial pyres offering death incinerated before inert idols, the prophet uses a pallet of perfumes to paint the penitent in all the aromas of life. The impression is of abounding growth and vitality. Never mind that the wandering rebel arrives unwashed, reeking of filth and stinking of death. The lost is found, the loved redeemed, received, restored, and beneath it all, bearing a distinctive scent only reminiscent of Lebanon.

Smells like Eden to me.

SATURDAY

He also told this parable to some who trusted in themselves that they were righteous and regarded others with contempt: "Two men went up to the temple to pray, one a Pharisee and the other a tax collector. The Pharisee, standing by himself, was praying thus, 'God, I thank you that I am not like other people: thieves, rogues, adulterers, or even like this tax collector. I fast twice a week; I give a tenth of all my income.' But the tax collector, standing far off, would not even look up to heaven, but was beating his breast and saying, 'God, be merciful to me, a sinner!' I tell you, this man went down to his home justified rather than the other; for all who exalt themselves will be humbled, but all who humble themselves will be exalted.

(Luke 18:9–14)

Smells a little fishy to me. That expression, or some variant of it, connotes suspicion. Luke tells us at the outset that the tale of the Pharisee and the tax collector is a parable addressing the judgmental notions that divide and separate us. A parable customarily avoids specific conclusion, thus when Luke appends an aphoristic tag line attributed to Jesus, my suspicions are aroused. I have no issue with Jesus's teaching; it's the context that smells "off."

The Pharisee's arrogance is counterpoised with the tax collector's groveling. Each man is an extreme stereotype and as such arouses my suspicion. As told by Luke, the story seems to imply that the characters in their extremes will simply exchange places.

If, as Jesus maintains, "all who exalt themselves will be humbled, but all who humble themselves will be exalted," God clearly abhors each extreme and is determined to draw us toward balance.

Moreover, as the exalted descend on the axis of humility and the humble ascend toward exaltation they may potentially meet, compelled from their extremes of estrangement and brought together.

Now that smells better.

LENT 4

SOUND

SUNDAY

The Creator is seldom glimpsed in Hebrew scripture, and even then is veiled, disguised. The voice, however, is prominent in scripture, where sound is the dominant medium in which God meets humankind. Speech, hearing, and listening represent the most tangible communion between God and us in verses recording songs sung in praise of God, petitions directed at the Divine to hear the prayers and listen to the pleas of the people. Just as urgently God presses the people to hear, to listen.

The auditory system is more expansive than we normally assume; listening and hearing are as much matters of the heart as of the ears. In Christian scripture Word is affirmed as Origin. A holy Conception is predicated upon the verbal announcement of an archangel who delivers a message, the response to which is a song, *Magnificat*.

Jesus, the principal messenger of God's good news, the Gospels, is as talkative as the Creator is taciturn. Preaching and parable flow freely from this incarnation and emissary of God, the Good Shepherd, whose voice is authority and assurance, guardian and guide to a people. When the flock passes to the stewardship of the apostles, and to Paul and his companions, letters dictated, transcribed, and read aloud connect communities.

Across the eons, and through the eras, all depends literally upon story, narrative communicated orally. Words passed from one to another until collected and arranged in silent symbols transcribed for travel. Story told in Galilee arrives in Rome, where the reader's eye, like silent voice, translates visible vocabulary, syntax, and punctuation into message and meaning.

Mining and discerning the depths of oral narrative and conversational speech Theodor Reik called "listening with the third ear." It's an apt description of an attentive hearing that distinguishes listening as a spiritual practice. Whether it be discursive meditation, the use of digital technology, music, art, cinema, reading, or any of the varied means by which we "hear," a spiritual practice of listening entails more than the mere intake of sound.

It's more akin to that combination of the auditory and anticipatory captured in the image of an expectant dog. Canine hearing isn't much sharper than human hearing; while the frequency range varies, dogs can and do go deaf. But the poise (and pose) of a dog in attentive wakefulness and alert waiting captures the spirit of anticipation that accompanies spiritual listening. The sound of the closing car door, the leather sole on the doorstep promise the return of the beloved.

Listening for God, listening to God, is an expectation that within recognizably familiar sounds—the reading of scripture, the poet's oral gift, the actors' lines, and every passing conversation—there awaits the possibility of the new, a doorway into deeper knowledge, more profound understanding, and more intimate relationship.

MONDAY

Now there was a royal official whose son lay ill in Capernaum. When he heard that Jesus had come from Judea to Galilee, he went and begged him to come down and heal his son, for he was at the point of death. Then Jesus said to him, "Unless you see signs and wonders you will not believe." The official said to him, "Sir, come down before my little boy dies." Jesus said to him, "Go; your son will live." The man believed the word that Jesus spoke to him and started on his way.

(John 4:46–50)

Word of mouth led the royal official to Galilee in search of help and hope. His son was back home in Capernaum, and deathly ill. He had heard of Jesus, his healing touch, and had rushed to find this wonder worker. Accustomed to such requests, Jesus responds with skepticism; he has seen this before. Nothing short of a demonstration of virtuoso miracle making will convince this desperate father who seems to confirm this hunch in his insistence that Jesus come to Capernaum immediately.

Jesus doesn't budge. Instead, he dismisses the petitioning father saying, "Go; your son will live." Surprising both Jesus and perhaps himself as well, "[t]he man believed the word that Jesus spoke and started on his way." The confidence in Jesus's assurance that the son would live convey sufficient hope to motivate his immediate return to home where, as he and we learn, his son awaits him, restored by word of mouth.

TUESDAY

God, . . . [q]uench our thirst with living water.

(from the Collect for Tuesday in the Fourth Week
of Lent, *Lesser Feasts and Fasts*, 2006, page 51)

Ezekiel traces water's course from the temple threshold
to the sea. The psalmist sings of roaring waters, heart-
gladdening streams. John recounts Jesus's encounter with
a sick man lying by a pool capable of cure in its stirred
waters. Today's readings gush with living water.

Living water. It's a descriptive term with multivalent
meaning. Living water: water in motion, filled with energy
and power sufficient to carry ships in its currents, to drown
pursuing enemy armies, to level whole cities in the path of
its roiling rampage.

Living water: water without which no human can long
survive, liquid essential to all living things on earth.

Living water: water made pure by the cleansing properties of clarifying passage over rock, oxygenated by droplets flung high and the mists of plunging falls, purged of contaminating poisons carrying death in stagnant pools.

Living water: water-given voice, singing fountains, gurgling streams, thunderous waves breaking on beaches.

Hear it?

WEDNESDAY

*Do not be astonished at this; for the hour is coming when
all who are in their graves will hear his voice and will
come out—those who have done good, to the resurrection of life, and those who have done evil, to the resurrection of condemnation.*

(John 5:28–29)

The dead hear? According to John, it happened to
Lazarus (John 11) and, even before John tells of
Lazarus, Jesus says it will happen to us.

I have long loved the notion that Lazarus responded to
the sound of his name, came forth from death when Jesus
beckoned. Yes, it's scary. Sufficiently frightening to spur
some to plot Jesus's death and set their plans in motion.

But strangely reassuring too. It is evidence not just of life
beyond death, but of more: evidence that one's personhood
remains immutable, that the name I was given at birth and

Baptism still serves to identify me. That I remain account-
able, responsible.

Whether beckoned with the affectionate tones of the
One seeking my company, or summoned by the One demanding an accounting, or likely a bit of both, the mere thought
of hearing that name when the great darkness descends and
fathomless silence engulfs seems ineffable grace, the sweet-
est music.

THURSDAY

The Lord said to Moses, "Go down at once!" . . . But Moses implored the LORD his God . . . [a]nd the LORD changed his mind.

(Exodus 32:7, 11, 14)

It was a stern order, probably the last thing Moses wanted to hear, that voice of God, white hot with rage dispatching him on a fool's errand. Moses is bold to respond, bolder to engage conversation, and boldest to argue with God.

I wonder what they sounded like, if it got heated as Moses and God went back and forth, speaking, listening, speaking, listening, talking over each other in a tangle of words until, finally, God relented and changed.

Was there a silence, one of those momentary rests in the score when the key shifts from minor to major, when God submitted to the power of persuasion?

That's the risk of conversation. The sound of syllables exchanged, the music of relationship, the soundtrack of growth and change.

FRIDAY

God, you have given us the Good News of your abounding love in your Son Jesus Christ: So fill our hearts with thankfulness that we may rejoice to proclaim the good tidings we have received . . .

(from the Collect for Friday in the Fourth Week of Lent, *Lesser Feasts and Fasts*, 2006, page 54)

My husband is hearing impaired. Even with fine hearing aids, comprehension of the spoken word is difficult. If he can watch the speaker's mouth as words are pronounced, he can more accurately receive the message. Projected captioning is even better.

The truth of God's love for us was articulated in many languages over many generations, but sound alone was insufficient. Combining the message with a messenger whose person fully embodied its meaning brought clarity and eventual comprehension to words worn smooth by repetition. Jesus proclaimed the gospel in his person, in being and living the words.

Thus we seek in prayer a relationship with God so substantial it shapes our own lives to conform with any and every syllable of the beautiful truth we're called to share, our lives so expressive that even those totally deaf to our voices nevertheless hear.

SATURDAY

On the last day of the festival, the great day, while Jesus was standing there, he cried out, "Let anyone who is thirsty come to me, and let the one who believes in me drink. As the scripture has said, 'Out of the believer's heart shall flow rivers of living water.'" . . . When they heard these words, some in the crowd said, "This is really the prophet." Others said, "This is the Messiah." But some asked, "Surely the Messiah does not come from Galilee, does he?"

(John 7:37–38, 40–41)

The incredulity is understandable; what the people were hearing didn't correspond to their expectations. It happens all the time. Sound can be deceptive, echoing, resonating, its source evasive or surprising. Hence the familiar caveat, "Consider the source."

Conceivably everyone with access to television or the internet has seen unexpectedly splendid musical debuts, when a plain, aging spinster in dowdy dress and sensible shoes, a stoop-shouldered laborer in work attire, or a diminutive child barely beyond kindergarten walks across a stage to a microphone in an auditorium filled to capacity, timidly responds to a few introductory questions, waits for the score's cue, opens their mouth, and offers a beautiful voice to the stunned crowd.

The incongruity challenges every expectation and arouses suspicion among some. Is this a trained professional cleverly costumed and foisted upon the gullible? Is this a hoax perpetrated by advanced sound technology and a talented lip-synch artist? Time will and does tell. This one is the real deal.

I'm a bit more sympathetic than John. I can understand those who struggled to align all they had been told and taught with what they were hearing, and from whom.

Jesus took them by surprise.

LENT 5

⁓

TASTE

SUNDAY

Cabs line a Chicago street not for fares but for food. Restaurants serving Middle Eastern food provide "home cooking" for the cabbies who congregate for cuisine, camaraderie, and conversation. Not far away, along a rather deserted block of low-slung nondescript commercial buildings, in every season and variant of weather, cabs and drivers are drawn by a food vendor's truck offering African fare, "comfort food" to workers seeking a taste of home.

Milk and honey, bread and wine are only a few of the many foods and flavors mentioned in biblical scripture and central to religious communities. Miraculous feedings and mundane meals pass through the mystic en route to the mythic as the divine is revealed on densely crowded hillsides, at a table in an upper room on the eve of crisis, in bread broken amid breaking hearts at day's end in Emmaus.

The soul's yearnings are described as a deep hunger, and union with God imagined as a table richly set by a Host who presides over the ultimate love feast, sufficient to sate and sustain for eternity.

Taste permeates the spiritual life. The central liturgies of many religions are meals, ritual tidbits and sips that, like the chef's complimentary *amuse bouche*, only whet the appetite for the more substantive celebrations of food and drink that nurture bodies and sustain cultures. We are people of the table.

Incarnation must be fed; bodies need food. A resurrected Jesus sharing a breakfast of freshly fried fish is a dish of many subtleties, each bite suffused with all the flavors of his life and story.

Sadly, abundance and accessibility of food don't always lead to spiritual fulfillment. The cabbies of my city remind me of the rich spirituality of food whose very aromas and flavors draw us to the curb, park us if only for a while, to sit at table with friend and kin. They help me recall church covered dish suppers, and funeral vigils, plates heaped with a community's love, balanced on laps, every forkful edible grace. Leisurely meals at table with family and friends, where the very anticipation of familiar tastes bound us in the Spirit's tether till the time to part arrived, when someone, leaning back would utter the benedictory acclamation, "That was just heavenly," met silently or aloud with a responsary "Amen."

MONDAY

Because they were elders of the people and judges, the assembly believed them.

(Susanna 41)

They said this to test him, so that they might have some charge to bring against him.

(John 8:6)

The readings appointed for today from Susanna (1–9, 15–29, 34–62) and John (8:1–11 or 8:12–20) recount unsavory stories: the attempted entrapment of Susanna by corrupt officials, the condemnation of the woman taken in adultery and objections of Jesus's detractors whose own sanctimoniousness comes down to us in the word "pharisaical."

These are tales whose telling can rightly be said to "leave a bad taste in the mouth."

Their modern counterpart is the sad reality of daily news reports of the corrupt use of power for sexual gratification and personal gain. Whether that power be the sway of adults over the underage or youth over the elderly, the clever over the simple, or any of the myriad instances wherein unfair advantage is taken, the injury is compounded by the perpetrators' attempts to impugn the character of the wronged. How can anyone be so crass?

The notion that I am somehow different, that I'm entitled, exempt—or at least more deserving? That certainly seems to be the attitude of those who, like Susanna's foes and the adulterer's accusers, feel that their office or status grants them an extra measure of credibility.

Truth suggests otherwise. Any standing I'm granted calls for a proportional humility. The old idiomatic expression "leaves a bad taste in the mouth" connotes an essential unfairness, an injustice. The counterpoise to unfairness is a scrupulous honesty about oneself, the kind that, like medicine, may taste bitter on first offering but brings sweet relief.

TUESDAY

". . . and we detest this miserable food."

(Numbers 21:5)

That's an add-on. One of those "and oh, by the way" comments of the type often appended to a lengthier complaint, as it is here, in a whining diatribe mounted by weary Israelites on exodus. Their anger and impatience with Moses has escalated; they are taking their complaint to the next level. They are angry with God. The "miserable food" of which they gripe is the manna God has provided for them, which adds an extra edge to the insult.

In crisis and deep pain, hunger's pangs are trumped. Dulled appetite makes food only another medication, fuel to sustain the suffering body.

When patients begin to complain about hospital food, it's sometimes an indication that their condition is improving, or that it's even time for them to go home.

Dissatisfaction with what God provides is endemic to a culture so obviously seeking more, and maybe an indication that it's time to get up, get out, and get on with our lives.

WEDNESDAY

Nebuchadnezzar was so filled with rage against Shadrach, Meshach, and Abednego that his face was distorted. He ordered the furnace to be heated up seven times more than was customary, and ordered some of the strongest guards in his army to bind Shadrach, Meshach, and Abednego and to throw them into the furnace of blazing fire. . . .

Then King Nebuchadnezzar was astonished and rose up quickly. He said to his counselors, "Was it not three men that we threw bound into the fire?" They answered the king, "True, O king." He replied, "But I see four men unbound, walking in the middle of the fire, and they are not hurt; and the fourth has the appearance of a god." Nebuchadnezzar then approached the door of the furnace of blazing fire and said, "Shadrach, Meshach, and Abednego, servants of the Most High God, come out! Come here!" So Shadrach, Meshach, and Abednego came out from the fire.

(Daniel 3:19–20, 24–26)

They've returned, those three faithful men named Hananiah, Mishael, and Azariah in Hebrew, but here identified by their Babylonian names, Shadrach, Meshach, and Abednego. Their refusal to bow down before the Babylonian idol worshipped by King Nebuchadnezzar has enraged the monarch. He spits his bitter-tasting anger in an order to fan the flames to a sevenfold increase in the furnace's temperature, so hot it proves fatal to the guards charged to bind and toss the rebels into the oven.

But the story takes a fascinating twist, reminiscent of Moses's experience before a different fire. Nebuchadnezzar gazes into the flames and discerns four figures where three have been consigned and none should survive. Amid the flames Shadrach, Meshach, and Abednego share communion with a figure bearing "the appearance of a god," described as an "angel," but clearly the Real Presence of their God.

By his reaction, we know that Nebuchadnezzar has tasted awe, wonder—the sacramental offering of three servants whose rebellious refusal of the king is rightly seen as fidelity, a profound trust validated and rewarded by the God whose potent protection delivers them from harm.

How sweet the words of a convinced convert whose mouth proclaims the goodness of God.

THURSDAY

"Whoever keeps my word will never taste death."

(John 8:52)

Clearly one meaning of this expression, likely the predominant meaning, is that those who are faithful will not experience death. But the translators have chosen an idiomatic option, imparting flavor.

It's an interesting choice. At the least, it qualifies the claim; since all mortals, including Jesus himself, experience death, the reality is unchallenged. There's no assurance, much less promise, that any escape death. Only that death will have no taste.

Death will be indiscriminate, but death will be indiscernible.

There's a consistent symmetry in this claim. I have no conscious memory of my birth. Passage from whatever preceded this life into this present realm was neither bitter nor sweet.

Perhaps the same will be true of my journey to the life beyond this one—that I may arrive, palate cleansed, ready to savor it all.

FRIDAY

Lord . . . [g]rant that we may accept with joy
the salvation you bestow, and manifest it to all the world
by the quality of our lives.

> (from the Collect for Friday in the Fifth Week
> of Lent, *Lesser Feasts and Fasts*, 2006, page 60)

I have become a laughingstock all day long;
> *everyone mocks me.*
For whenever I speak, I must cry out,
> *I must shout, "Violence and destruction!"*

> (Jeremiah 20:7–8)

It is not for a good work that we are going to stone you,
but for blasphemy . . .

> (John 10:33)

Visiting foreign cousins for the first time on their soil,
I sat down to a meal lovingly prepared and proudly

served. Most was quite good, but one item was quite strange, with a texture and taste I struggled but barely succeeded in sampling, so as to signify appreciation for the love it represented.

Taste is a sense of what is appropriate, lovely, acceptable, or esthetically pleasing. Like its physical counterpart, this taste is subjective. What one person or culture finds pleasing to the palate or the social, religious, or political sensibilities may be deemed offensive by another.

Poor Jeremiah laments that at least some of the burden of his vocation is the tackiness of his prophecy. He is mocked and demeaned because he's saddled with a message of gloom and doom amid a people who want only affirmation. It's not easy to be countercultural, in his era or ours.

Jesus risks stoning because his claims are deemed irreverent, lacking in proper piety. He is charged with blasphemy because he dares to assert that ordinary humanity is endowed with an essential holiness; the suggestion that a human can claim kinship with God is base profanity.

Even our prayer today hints at our discomfort with God's demanding gospel; surely an attractive salvation would be joyfully, eagerly acceptable. Instead, God's salvation sometimes needs a divine nudge and grace to accept, that our message be tastefully set forth in "the quality of our lives."

SATURDAY

Lord, . . . [l]ook with favor . . . upon those who in these Lenten days are being prepared for Holy Baptism.

(from the Collect for Saturday in the Fifth Week of Lent, *Lesser Feasts and Fasts*, 2006, page 61)

Thus says the Lord GOD: I will take the people of Israel from the nations among which they have gone, and will gather them from every quarter, and bring them to their own land. I will make them one nation in the land, on the mountains of Israel; and one king shall be king over them all. Never again shall they be two nations, and never again shall they be divided into two kingdoms.

(Ezekiel 37:21–22)

The picture of unity presented in Ezekiel's prophecy is lacking only one thing: where's the food? That great homecoming, when a long divided people is reconciled, settled and secure in one place under one ruler wants only food and drink to be a perfect party.

Thus on this final day of Lent, the collect points us toward Baptism, celebrated by some and renewed by all Christians on Easter. We're reminded that we're only now in preparation, and our lectionary adheres to that old theatrical axiom, "always leave them wanting more."

We're not there yet. Our senses are stimulated and we're hungry, eager to enjoy. But we've more journey to make en route to Easter, where the feast awaits.

HOLY WEEK

PALM SUNDAY

Isaiah (50:4–9) reminds us that God has given the prophet—and each of us—tongues, ears, faces, and feelings. The psalmist (Psalm 31) laments an eye, throat, and belly "consumed with sorrow," physical loss, and emotional grief. The Epistle (Philippians 2:5–11) admonishes to "[l]et the same mind be in you that was in Christ Jesus," an invitation to active empathy. The Gospel, each year from a different Gospel writer's perspective, lays out the entire sad story, the terrain and trajectory of our travels this week spread before us like the map laid out in preparation "that we may walk in the way of [Jesus's] suffering" en route to his resurrection, the journey described in the collect.

Palm Sunday is symbolically complex. Its pace and complexity most approximate the kind of days that we live, in a rushed, stimulating world. All the senses are called into service as we enter empathically into the story of God's life and work among us. Throughout a Lent of sensory exploration and reflection, we've prepared for this week.

Palm Sunday is presumably about palm branches, symbols of victory. But those branches are named for foliage mimicking fingers radiating from a central point—like our hands, whose inner surfaces are made to receive and to hold.

Hands are central to the drama we rehearse in the gospel every year on this day. Heads and hearts play their roles, for religion is usually a matter of one organ or the other, of intellect or sentiment. But the true religion's in the hands, in what and how one touches. With our palms we eucharistic peoples commune with God. Into our hands the bread is placed, the cup taken.

The heart can pain, pine, and even break over homelessness, or disease, or injustice, or abuse. The mind grows exhausted in contemplating the complexities of economic, political, and social systems that spawn the seemingly endless stream of life's litany. But the true religion is in the hands that feed and clothe and shelter, that tenderly tend the sick, that bring healing to abused and abuser alike.

Jesus returns to Jerusalem, from which he had been banished under threat of stoning, or worse. In returning to Jerusalem, Jesus is given into our hands—human hands.

His disciples drop their hands and curl them in sleep—all but the one who didn't rest, whose hands embraced Jesus and delivered him to hands eagerly waiting to seize him. When finally roused, another takes up a sword, making mayhem where mending was needed—then denies ever having known Jesus, wipes his hands of the very faith that had filled them.

The priests palm Jesus off on the government, who send him back after leaving the marks of their hands in lashes and thorns. On his way to be crucified, soldiers press the burdensome cross into the hands of Simon of Cyrene. They drive their spikes through Jesus's empty palms, severing the so-called lifelines that intersect in the folds, and hanging him up to die, roll dice in their palms, and finger the fine textures of the robe he'd worn.

While Jesus is in pain and delirium, crying out in thirst, even the mother who had held him in her hands can't lift a hand to help, nor dare. An unnamed stranger's hands soak the sponge in vinegar and pitifully attempt to revive the ebbing life, or only ease the pain.

Even in the end it's not accustomed hands or familiar ones that receive his body: Joseph of Arimathaea takes it into his hands to visit Pilate, and it's into his and Nicodemus's hands the body is finally and yet first delivered—Nicodemus, the last anyone would expect to become the first to commune, fulfilling Jesus's own teaching.

From hand to hand, from life to death, from then to now.

The true religion is in the hands.

Monday

Six days before the Passover Jesus came to Bethany, the home of Lazarus, whom he had raised from the dead. There they gave a dinner for him. Martha served, and Lazarus was one of those at the table with him. Mary took a pound of costly perfume made of pure nard, anointed Jesus's feet, and wiped them with her hair. The house was filled with the fragrance of the perfume. But Judas Iscariot, one of his disciples (the one who was about to betray him), said, "Why was this perfume not sold for three hundred denarii and the money given to the poor?"

(John 12:1–5)

The flurry of attention generated by Jesus's return to Jerusalem celebrated in yesterday's Palm Sunday rites gives way today to a quieter scene in a more private setting. Wisely adopting a lower profile, Jesus is depicted in John's Gospel among his closest friends—Mary, Martha, and Lazarus—at the table in their house at Bethany. Of the disciples, we know that Judas at least is present.

While a strictly literal chronology may not apply to the placement of this episode in this week's order, it feels right to balance yesterday's dangerous public display with this intimate scene among trusted companions. The story is a feast for the senses. It is a dinner and presumably something of a feast freed from the bounds of the prescribed diet of formal religious ritual. Because his friends have prepared the dinner especially for him, the table was likely set with his favorite dishes, "comfort food" for the journey ahead.

And there's more. There is the rich perfume of the anointing oils, and the sanctimonious stink raised by Judas's objections—a subtle reminder of the darker pall being gradually drawn over Jesus's life.

Between the extremes of relaxing food and anointing massage and the tense anger of Judas's outburst, there's the enigmatic Lazarus, silent bridge between the realms of human experience and incarnate reminder that "in the midst of life we are in death" (The Book of Common Prayer, Service for Burial, page 484).

TUESDAY

Jesus answered them, ". . . Very truly, I tell you, unless a grain of wheat falls into the earth and dies, it remains just a single grain; but if it dies, it bears much fruit. Those who love their life lose it, and those who hate their life in this world will keep it for eternal life. . . ."

Jesus said to them, "The light is with you for a little longer. Walk while you have the light, so that the darkness may not overtake you. If you walk in the darkness, you do not know where you are going. While you have the light, believe in the light, so that you may become children of light."

After Jesus had said this, he departed and hid from them.

(John 12:23–25, 35–36)

The palpable honesty in today's Gospel hits like a stinging slap. How brutally frank Jesus is in his open confession of his own discomfort and uneasiness in a moment of

118

important witness to the curious Greeks who have sought him out. Led by Philip and Andrew, those Gentile seekers must surely have been taken aback by Jesus's blunt realism.

Presumably, they had been drawn to Jesus by tales of his charismatic preaching and winning personality, by his wise parables and his healing ways. The harsh realities of life and death are laid out by Jesus with bracing candor, followed by the admission framed rather like a dramatic aside allowing only a select audience access to his true inner struggle, "My soul is troubled." Jesus continues in a prayer-like dialogue with God, seeking clarity in the midst of profound vocational uncertainty and provoking a thunderous affirmation of the truth Jesus is presenting: "a voice came from heaven, 'I have glorified it, and I will glorify it again.'"

Whether the vocal affirmation was audible or not is moot. Some truths falling upon our ears strike so resonantly against our own experience it's as though all Creation responds with a resounding, congregational "Amen."

Yet even Jesus is unsure of what to say, how far to go. By the end of his extemporaneous open reflection in conversation with the crowd, he's caught up in the moment until he himself hears what he's saying, and convicted by his own words, he doesn't simply depart. He withdraws, and seized by the shock of his own bold frankness, he hides.

WEDNESDAY

Jesus was troubled in spirit, and declared, "Very truly, I tell you, one of you will betray me." The disciples looked at one another, uncertain of whom he was speaking. One of his disciples—the one whom Jesus loved—was reclining next to him; Simon Peter therefore motioned to him to ask Jesus of whom he was speaking. So while reclining next to Jesus, he asked him, "Lord, who is it?" Jesus answered, "It is the one to whom I give this piece of bread when I have dipped it in the dish." So when he had dipped the piece of bread, he gave it to Judas son of Simon Iscariot. After he received the piece of bread Satan entered into him. Jesus said to him, "Do quickly what you are going to do."

(John 13:21–27)

The narrative is out of sequence again today. This passage relates a detail from John's Gospel that proceeds out of the foot washing, the focus of tomorrow's reading and rite. But in this placement it serves as a dramatic rumination, as though Jesus is thinking through what lies ahead, preparing himself to respond to an anticipation too complex to be left to spontaneous reflex.

He knows if only intuitively that betrayal is likely; how might he offer and invite open confrontation with his accuser and, more importantly, if the invitation is enjoined, how shall he respond?

That he was "troubled in spirit" puts the matter far too lightly. Anyone who has been in a like situation well knows this heart-racing anxiety.

But Jesus has reflected long and hard on this critical moment. It is his one opportunity to validate the sanctity of freedom—even, especially, the freedom to make a deadly, murderous mistake—and his only chance to extend personal absolution to an enemy.

He doesn't ask for confession; he seeks communion. He and his opponent will share bread and wine. It's the only version of the sacramental meal in John's telling, a powerful image of friend and foe holding the wine-sopped bread between them.

There's no indication that either ate.

MAUNDY THURSDAY

[D]uring supper Jesus . . . got up from the table, took off his outer robe, and tied a towel around himself. Then he poured water into a basin and began to wash the disciples' feet and to wipe them with the towel that was tied around him.

(John 13:2–5)

John's Gospel omits the topic of conversation around the table, but there must've been some sense that things were reaching a critical moment, that the action they'd all signed on for was about to break loose into some revolutionary upheaval. Judas had left, taking some of the tension, but leaving much preoccupation among them. Surely, as other Gospels portray them, they indulged flights of fantasy, visions of success, and perhaps even a few nightmarish fears of failure.

Jesus, too, was distracted, as any of us would be under those circumstances. His mind and heart were running and rerunning all the tapes of all the possible scenarios taking place beyond that room. He needed something to anchor him to the moment, bring him back to the present and to them. Girding himself with a towel, he knelt and began to wash their feet. A simple, mundane act of hospitality grounded him, and them.

It wasn't a mandate so much as a gift. "This is what I do for you," are the words that one version has Jesus say.

Jesus knew that the way ahead of him was his alone and that each of the others with him had been called by God to walk other paths. He really didn't expect them to accompany him all the way; he promised not that they would always be together as a group, but that wherever they went hereafter he'd be with them.

So he literally put his hand in, gave them this labor of the servant, washing their feet. It was a gift that could go with them wherever they went, a gift they would remember every time they took a step, or stubbed a toe, massaged a cramp or removed their shoes—which is to say, a gift for the everyday. It was a gift that left them wondering, and kept them pondering, feeding their minds and filling their hearts.

But it was a gift to him as well. Down on the floor, as he grasped each ankle, cradled, bathed, and dried each foot, he was joined by touch to each of them, driven by the same instinct that would later move Mary to reach for him in the garden path. Couldn't he just remain there, kneeling, giving?

The greater, harder labor was the rising.

GOOD FRIDAY

Almighty God . . . behold this your family.

(from the Collect for Good Friday,
The Book of Common Prayer, page 221)

The entire story is told today. The narrative is highly descriptive, sensual, beyond the rational, in the realm of pure experience. It's a strangely noticeable departure in John's Gospel, a text more usually associated with intellectual theology than with emotional drama.

This is high drama, with vibrant action and a full orchestra of human emotion. Led by Judas, soldiers, police, priests, and others burst into the opening scene. There are "lanterns, torches, and weapons"—all potential hazards in a confused melee.

Jesus attempts to minimize the danger, stepping forward and asking for clarity in the noise and jostling. When he affirms that he is the one they seek, they are not described as "taken aback" by Jesus's self-identification, but are choreographed in surprise as they step back and fall to the ground.

Jesus asks again whom they seek and this time they move to arrest him, provoking Peter's impetuous defense in drawing Malchus's blood. Thereafter follows a rapidly shifting tale that moves us from scenes of Peter's private fear and betrayal just beyond the courtyard where Annas and Caiaphas examine Jesus; back to Peter and another denial; to the court of Pilate, to the public release of Barabbas; to the flogging and soldiers' mockery; to continued debate between the religious and political figures; to the pavement of Gabbathta where on this eve of Passover the sentence is pronounced and moves the action to a prolonged execution involving a vinegar sop and a deep sword thrust to guarantee death in time to comply with ritual demands, while the attention swings from gambling soldiers to mourning friends and relatives; to the tender scene of Nicodemus and Joseph of Arimethea anointing the corpse and laying it to rest in the tomb.

Not until the invention of cameras capable of recording action could such a story be so vividly enacted and compactly told. In lieu of actual images, we encounter a story written for our imaginations. We hear its words and cadences and descriptions of physical encounters involving the full array of human experience and emotion—dark and light, heat and cold, life and death.

Yet, oddly, our prayer invites God to behold us, God's family. God is invited to watch us as we engage the dramatic story of our salvation. In an ironic reversal, on this day so filled with words we recite no creed and rehearse few prayers. Today God isn't asked to hear us, but to look at us.

What, pray tell, is written on our faces, upon our lives?

HOLY SATURDAY

I've long appreciated this day as one of quiet absence.
Where the Eucharist is shared on Good Friday, the elements are consumed from sacramental reserves and prop-
erly depleted, leaving an empty tabernacle or aumbry.
Symbolically, Christ has died and is not among us.

Inviting and allowing that absence to pervade this particular day honors the sense, and sensibility, of Christian
liturgy. "Were you there when they crucified my Lord?" asks
the old spiritual (*Hymnal 1982*, 172). If one is truly present
to Good Friday, it's only right that we feel the profound loss
of that day's realities, the holy hangover of Holy Saturday.

On this day our senses are filtered through emotional
loss. Grief dulls the appetite. Sadness alters the visual perspective. The silencing of a familiar voice ushers a palpable
hush. Flowers intended for open gardens smell different
within funereal confines. In the absence of the beloved,
the warmth of another's embrace assures connection with

the world, affirms the possibilities of hope, and allows the release of pain that assaults our every vulnerability.

Yet loss is also clarifying. In the presence and practices of human mortality, standing in the bright light of a cemetery, the world—like a room from which a familiar chair has been taken away—looks different. Any and every removal only heightens awareness of what remains. An alteration in essential relationship changes one's responsibilities.

Feeling, sensing the difference between yesterday and today is the bridge to every tomorrow.

EASTER DAY

Almighty God . . . [g]rant that we . . . may be raised from
the death of sin by your life-giving Spirit.

(from the Collect for Easter Day,
The Book of Common Prayer, page 222)

I have no memory of life before my birth, nor of the birth
itself. I presume, as live birth is often depicted, I was grasped
by the ankles and lifted to clear my respiratory passages to
admit that initial gasp of earthly air. In that breath, my sensate awareness began. That first breath was the life-giving
spirit from which all my experience of this life proceeded.

At the sound of his familiar voice pronouncing her
name, Mary is said to have uttered a single word, *Rabbouni*.
But between the sound of Jesus's voice and hers, in that
split-second recognition, Mary had to breathe.

Given the circumstances, I can only imagine that she
gasped, as any of us would in the same situation. She inhaled

quickly in a reflex action, a response to the surprise of the risen friend before her.

"Inspire" is an old, little-used word for "inhale." In this instance, it is the perfect word, for Mary's response to the reality of the risen Jesus is genuine inspiration—literally, inhalation. Moreover, it is an inhalation incorporating the several dimensions of that word, including inspiration's imparting the ability to feel.

In that sharp, gasping intake, Mary inhaled the Resurrection and it was a life-giving breath.

If the "death of sin" is the tragic separation from God that deadens the human spirit, the gasp of recognition when one truly takes in the fullness of the Resurrection, the realization of full reunion with God—that nothing can ever separate us from the God who loves us—is the first breath of real life.

It's only natural that she grabbed him. The one she had lost had been found; Mary's instinct was to grab and hold tight lest she lose again. But Jesus wouldn't be bound, certainly not by any fear.

In the bracing air of Resurrection, each inhaled God's life-giving Spirit. No fear or shame to burden them, no angelic sentries guarding passage, extending from where they stood into all eternity, a Creation filled with God's abundance was ready for them.

They were free to go.